Eh Yup! how are yer? Is what a Sheffielder using the local dialect, might say to someone they know as a casual greeting, and to ask about their health. Their reply, using the same dialect, would be;- "Am allreet ta" which means;- "I am fine thanks."

This unique dialect is still used by some Sheffielders, and has become one of Sheffield's spoken "secrets."

It is hardly surprising that visitors to the city struggle to understand what is being said, so we have included some local phrases with a translation, plus cartoons in this book. This is so everyone can have a go at speaking what is locally called;- "Sheffieldish."

*(The examples in this book have been written to aid the pronunciation)*

Sheffield, has many other "secrets" that even the city residents might not be aware of. To aid the reader, we have included a brief description of the featured item, and a postcode, so that they can be easily visited.

They are all available to see at the time of writing this book, and can be viewed at leisure, or perhaps as a competition between family members to see who can find them all first?

The people of Sheffield are proud of their city and their heritage, and it is with our thanks that we include some of their pictures, stories and their memories, in this latest edition.

We hope you enjoy it!

Upper Chapel - (S1 2LG)
*"Mother and Child" bronze by George Fullard, was originally created in 1956, using plaster!*

"By 'eck," the old folk would say to us kids, "Thas never 'ad it so good," and they would soon follow that by recalling how hard times had been for them when they were young. It is only now that I have my own children, I can see what they meant, as life was very different in Sheffield during the 1960's compared to the present day.

It was a time when cars and televisions were rare luxury items, and parking meters, mobile phones, and video games had yet to be invented. Some memories from those meagre times follow.

As a child, during the 1960's, the only parts of the city centre I knew were;- Dixon Lane, The Moor, and the "Rag and Tag" markets, because that was were we did most of our city shopping. It was always busy, and bustling with shoppers, tramcars, and traders.

Everyone appeared oblivious to the noise and smog from the steelworks, and the strong smell of malt and hops coming from the Whitbread brewery.

*The River Don from Lady's Bridge*

I liked to look over the wall at Lady's bridge into the murky, yellow, River Don that was tainted by steel waste, and discarded junk. There was no chance of ever seeing a fish, but there was a chance of seeing one of the "big rats" running along the river bank, that some people said were as big as a cat.

*The Sheaf Market in the 1960's*

On Friday afternoons, the markets were full of people looking for bargains. Some women had already been to their husbands workplace to collect their pay packet. (Steelworkers would throw their pay packets from the factory window to their wives waiting to catch them below.)

This was a smart move to beat the crowds, and to prevent the wage being spent on ale by their husbands.

*Reduced meat prices at the weekend*

The big city centre stores such as;- Redgates toyshop, Cole's, Walsh's, Atkinson's, and the Castle House Co-op, attracted the shoppers in droves by supplying home furnishings and the larger household appliances.

The supermarkets as we know them now, had yet to be built, and because very few people owned cars, most people relied heavily on the convenience of the "Corner shop" for their everyday food.

The city centre was slowly changing, yet where I lived at Walkley, appeared to be a place that was always the same, and frozen in time.

I recall as a child, that it was perfectly normal to be sent to the corner shop to buy half a pound of loose biscuits, or to ask for ten Park Drive fags (cigarettes) "for me dad." If we ran out of butter, I was sent to buy another slice, which was cut off a large block, weighed, and priced per ounce.

*Eatin' spice (sweets)*

Sometimes my Grandma called round, and would ask me to buy her some sweets whilst I was going. She always had the same, which was;- 4 oz. of chocolate limes. I would usually get one of them for going. She would enjoy the sweets in her comfy chair, listening to "The Archers" on her valve radio.

As kids, we would always play on the streets, occupying our time playing tiggy, skipping, hula hoops, or whipping spinning tops. We loved autumn and the Conker season, as it was a change to our normal games. Having no television, we learnt to make do with simple pleasures.

When playing outside in the street, we were always alert in case we ran into a Mod, Rocker or Skinhead gang. Bullying for the sake of it and to be "feighting in't street," was fairly common back then.

*Dus tha wanna feight?*

Our house in Walkley, was a red brick terraced house, and like many others at that time, had an outside toilet and had no internal bathroom. Hung on our outside wall was our tin bath, which was brought inside into the living room on bath days.

Our back door faced the neighbours, and we shared a common yard. Our garden was very small, and had the remains of an Anderson shelter in it. (Air raid shelter)

We shared a washing pole with our next door neighbour, but we had separate lines.

*WESHIN Line - Washing line*

Clothes washing used to be complicated back then, and was a five stage process. Stubborn stains were first removed by rubbing the clothes on a ribbed wooden board next to the sink. Next, the dirty clothes would be manually agitated by using a wooden stick, in a hot water tub containing a sprinkling of soap powder. Once the clothes were clean, they were rinsed in the tub with fresh clean water. The clothes were then dragged out of the washer tub and put into a basket, ready to pass through the mangle outside. Finally, the clothes were hung on the washing line with wooden pegs to dry.

Our house had a coal fire that had to be made each morning to warm the house. An ornamental "Knight" holding assorted fire tools was next to the coal scuttle on the hearth. To get the fire started, I had to use the tools, coal, firelighters and a newspaper. A full double page was spread across the chimney to get the updraft going, but on occasions the paper caught fire, and it had to be thrown quickly into the fire. The fireguard was always in place when the fire was lit, as the hot cokes would sometimes crack loudly and jump out of the fire and onto the carpet, like a mini volcano.

Like our neighbour, we had a Yorkshire range in the main dining room. (Photo right) The kitchen was where all the food was prepared, but anything for roasting or boiling, was cooked on the range.

The range also provided hot water from a kettle sitting on the fire plate, but we were lucky to also have an ASCOT hot water geyser in the kitchen. It was faster, but scared me to death when it fired up!

"Chuck the cat anuther goldfish" - term of extravagance

Living in back to back houses with shared yards, inevitably meant that you would meet your neighbour or the people at the bottom of the yard - especially on washdays.

It was a very close-knit community back then, and the latest gossip was exchanged about people's family troubles, joys, births, deaths, work, and how they lost their shirt on the horses. Mandatory topics included in all conversations, were peoples love life, and any ailments they were suffering from.

It appeared to me at the time, that people actually got some sort of free therapy when they moaned and complained to each other about how hard life was for them.

*Worrabout - What about*

The thing I often moaned about was having to distemper the outside toilet. I was given a pot full of watery white "paint" to put on the walls, which when dry, flaked. I was terrified of brushing my clothes against it, because it always left white powdery marks on them.

Another chore whilst in the toilet, was to check the paraffin stove for fuel, which was our frost protection for the lead water pipe.

There was also a monthly maintenance task to do on the Yorkshire Range. I had to apply a type of black lead polish to keep it from rusting, and to cover up the burn marks.
It was a messy job, but it did make it look like new again.

*Loys yer shirt - skint*

Perhaps, a lot of things we all did back then will appear odd today, but due to the lack of money, we had little choice.
That way of life slowly changed with time, and what was then normal, lapsed into a forgotten and secret world of its own.

Some examples of the "hard times" follow...

*Poorly TOO'ER - TOE hurts*

## The Money Secrets

Obtaining money was perhaps harder back then, as many wages tended to be low, there were no ATM's, no easily available credit cards, and getting a bank overdraft was like a Spanish Inquisition.

Many poorer families were compelled to juggle their finances to get money in, and prevent paying it out.

How they did it was a closely guarded family secret, kept even from friends and in particular, the inquisitive neighbours. The children were also sworn to secrecy, with dire consequences for them if they told anyone of the families hardships.

*In yer dreams - no chance*

\*\*\*

It was fairly common for children to get their school uniforms "On the tick," which was a form of credit offered by some garment sellers. They would add up the cost of the clothes you were taking, and give you a weekly payment book.

There was a degree of shame being seen to do this, so we would wait across the road from the shop to check the coast was clear,- before going in.

*On't tick - On weekly credit*

\*\*\*

Children knew they could always make some "sweet money" by searching the dustbins on collection day.

To find a pop bottle in the bins and return it to the sweet shop would pay you 2D. This was equivalent to 16 Black Jacks, or 8 "Flying Saucers," or a Sherbet Dip.

As there was always three or four pop bottle "Searchers" in our gang, we would always pool what we found, and share the sweets amongst us all.

*Pop bottle profits*

Buying furniture from the city centre stores was often done on a credit type basis, and their cash collectors would knock on your door late Friday evening (as it was pay day) to make sure that they got their repayment.

At our house, it was always a matter of "Robbing Peter to pay Paul," and it was not unusual for us to draw all the curtains early Friday evening. We would all dive behind the settee if we heard the garden gate open.

Crouching in silence, we could see the shadow of a man trying to find a peep hole between the curtains to try and catch us out. It was terrifying but necessary, and even though our parents called it hide and seek, we knew different.

*Hide 'n seek*

\*\*\*

Money was saved on buying toilet paper by cutting up a newspaper into small squares, putting a hole in one corner, and tying it onto a string loop. It could then be hung on a nail in the outside toilet - ready for use.

\*\*\*

*Toilet paper - literally!*

Our outside toilet like many others, had a toilet seat that consisted of a large plank of varnished wood, with a large hole in the centre. It looked medieval, but when you wanted to go, you didn't care!

\*\*\*

Trousers with holes in the knee (which is now fashionable) was then considered to be worn out. To save money and make them respectable again, we took off the back pocket to patch over the holes.

In Bay City Roller fashion days, the trouser legs could be cut up the seams and a tartan triangle sown in to make it a fashionable flared trouser. This upgrade cost a fraction of the fashion clothes in the city centre.

*Tartan Flared Jeans*

# Sheffield Life

More examples of Sheffield life, and their money saving ideas follow on this page.

*"Ere's tuppence for yer bus fare, and don't walk there and spend it on penny buns and sweets."*
*(Irene)*

\*\*\*

*"We used to make pegged rugs. We would split a peg in half, put a point on it and then use it to weave rags through an oblong piece of old sack. It looked great when it was done, and it was easy to clean as well."* *(Ivy)*

\*\*\*

*"I've packed you up dripping cakes for school, and I've put plenty of jelly and salt on them for you. That'll grease yer chest!"* *(Flo)*

\*\*\*

*"Yer can ave chicklin and bag wi bread n butter or a pigs trotter for yer tea - which is it?"* *(Anon)*

\*\*\*

*"There have been some great things on the tip this week. I've brought home a set of pram wheels for a Go Kart, and an old bike frame that I can do up and flog!" (Sell)* *(Chris)*

\*\*\*

*"Mam....I've gorra big ole in't borrum o' me shoer!" was usually replied to by;- "Cut another piece of cardboard out and put it inside yer shoe."*
*Which was in turn replied by;- "I did that last week and the week before!"*
*"Yer getting good at doing it then?" Mam replied cockily.*
*I wanted to mention "cobblers" in my reply to her - but didn't.*

3D bus ticket

Dripping cakes

Profitable week

Ole in me SHOER

**"Mam, thurs an ole in me shoer" - Mum, I have a hole in my shoe**

I remember in the 1970's, using the "Hole in the road" pedestrian underpass that connected Angel Street, Commercial Street, High Street, and Arundel Gate.

In the underpass was a large fish tank filled with various fish.

It was a very popular meeting place. "Meet you at the fish tank." *(CW)*

***

*Gurra Post Office forus wiltha luv, and gerrus a 50P book o' stamps?*

*Or*

*Will you go to the Post Office and get me a 50P book of stamps?*
*(1980's)*

50p

Royal Mail Stamps

One at 14p
Three at 11½p
One at 1p
One at ½p

### Donkey Stone fer yer rags!

Donkey Stone was a scouring stone that took its name from the trade mark of one of the earliest firms to produce it;- Reads of Manchester.

It was originally used in the mills of Lancashire and Yorkshire, to put a none slip surface on the greasy mill steps.

It soon became a trade offering from the "Rag and Bone" man in exchange for household rags. The stones were used by housewives to "stone" the front door step with a white edging. This not only became a safety feature for dark nights, but a form of competition on the streets between housewives, to see who had the nicest doorsteps. It was even applied to window sill edges. The practice ended when the stone production ceased.

# Sheffield Trams

I am perhaps fortunate when I was a young child, to have rode on the old Sheffield trams. I used to travel frequently with my mother from the Crookes tram terminus on Pickmere Road, to High Street in the town centre.

The trams had a unique charm about them with their wooden seats, ringing bells, and the deep rumbling noises coming from the tracks.

The tram era came to an end in the 1960's, with the introduction of the new motor buses. The old tram tracks (as seen in the second photo) were being systematically removed as the routes closed.

The last trams ran between Leopold Street and Beauchief on 8th October 1960.

Many of the old unwanted trams, went down specially laid tracks, that went directly into Thomas Ward's scrap yard. Thankfully, some of Sheffield's old tramcars are preserved at the Crich Tramway museum.

Perhaps the trams took some "secrets" with them to the scrap yard, that are not seen on the modern Supertrams, such as:-

• Signs were displayed inside the old trams telling the passengers - "No spitting."
This was necessary because steelworkers were known to clear their throats and noses of steel dust, by spitting it on the floor.

• At the terminus, the tram driver had to change the trams direction by pulling on a rope to swing around the electric trolley pole. He would also have to go down the inside of the tram, flipping the wooden seat backs, so they faced the opposite way.

• The earlier trams did not have any doors on them, and people would literally jump on and off - even when the tram was moving.

Stagecoach

SUPERTRAM

# "Tha talks reet funny"

By Chris Whomersley

They say Yorkshire folk they "talk reet funny"
using words like "brass" instead o' money.
If "narthenthee" really means "now then you"
What does a visitor to Yorkshire do?

They rack their brains, and their faces turn red,
Cus it'aint their fault they wern't born and bred,
In God's Yorkshire where they'd understand,
It's the finest place throughout the land.

Our dialect is special and down to earth,
Outsiders try to speak it - to our mirth.
It's our secret code and we're proud orit,
Joinin' up words and makinem fit.

It's the way it is, and its through evolution
Hard manual graft helped forge this solution.
It is worrit is and it didn't take us long,
To make up words so it rolls off the tongue.

We've created new words wi 'out any space,
But they've gorra be spoken wi' a straight face.
Say it tight lipped wi' a fag in yer gob,
and show no emotion and youv'e done the job.

If they don't know what yer meant, no need to worry,
Repeat it slowly then say you are sorry,
that words like Ey lad, bereet and gerrusanother,
can only be understood by a Yorkshire brother.

We're proud of our dialect and worrit's become,
t 'aint our fault tharrits not understood by some.
But there is one way you could end all the fuss,
Move to Yorkshire and be one of us!

# Dus tha know tha Pubs?

**The Ship Inn** - Shalesmoor. S3 8UL

The inn dates back to around 1750. In the Sheffield flood on 11th March 1864, two seamen staying at the inn drowned as they tried to escape the flood in the secret tunnels beneath the Inn. Ghost sightings down in the cellar, may be linked to this event?

**The Mucky Duck?**          S3 8NA

It was an important music venue in the 1960's, with bands playing here such as AC/DC, Genesis, The Clash, Sex Pistols and Buzzcocks to name a few. The venues name has been;- The Black Swan, The Complete Angler, The Mucky Duck, and The Boardwalk Nightclub.

**The Old Queens Head.**     S1 2BG

Dating from around 1475, it is the oldest building in the city centre.
It may once have been used as the Earls hunting lodge for wildfowl in the nearby ponds. (Now gone) .
The pub is likely to be named after Mary, Queen of Scots, and it was given Grade II* status in 1952.

**The Noose & Gibbet Inn**    S9 2DE

The inn features Spence Broughton who robbed mail from a stagecoach on Attercliffe common.
He was sentenced in 1792 for the crime, and was hung and gibbeted. His body was left on display for over 27 years, as a deterrent to others.

"It's so cold - brass monkeys are lookin fer welders" - its freezing

# Birley Spa Bath House

"Burh-ley" is of Saxon origin, and means;- "defence and clearing."
The Birley Spa Bath house and grounds, is found in secluded woodland just off Birley Spa Lane, in the S12 Hackenthorpe district of Sheffield.

A book by Platt in the 1930's, mentions that the earliest establishment of a spa on this site was around the early 1700's, and was built by a Quaker called Sutcliffe. This square bathing facility existed until 1793, when the bath became unused, and it was filled in with stones.

Around 1843, Earl Manvers, the Viscount of Newark, and patron and appropriator of Beighton, and owner of the spa, started to develop the site for up market clientele that wanted to "take the waters."
A chemist from Leeds had been to test the waters, and found them to be beneficial.

The bath house building shown here, dates from 1843, and was then called the Bath Hotel. Inside, there were plunge and shower baths, with a variety of tariffs and options. There was even a charity set up so that the poor could use the facilities.

*Earl Manver's crest*

The spa reached the height of its fame in the 1860's, but it failed to make a profit up to 1878, which led to the hotel closure.
The last bath remained in use up to 1895.

Just prior to WWI, the spa waters had ceased to flow. This was possibly due to the extensive coal mining in the area, and the diverting of the spa water elsewhere.

*The Plunge Bath*

During the 1920-30's, the area was used as a pleasure ground, featuring swings, roundabouts, a fishpond and an aerial flight. It was an ideal place for people to go and relax.
In 1939, at the start of the war, the grounds were closed and the area fell into decline.

In 1966, the Spa buildings were partially restored, and it is now used for special events, and as a community centre.

*The Bath House*

# Painted Fabrics Ltd. 1915 - 1959

Perhaps one of Sheffield's best kept secrets was a company called Painted Fabrics? I have lived in Sheffield all my life, and I had never heard of it, but by chance I was enlightened by Mr. Des Brooks, who told me of its history and how it was formed.

During the First World War, some soldiers survived near-death events, but sustained body disfigurements and suffered from mental shock. They would spend months in hospital recovering, only to find that on their release, no one wanted to employ them due to their loss of limbs and poor mobility. A magazine at the time summed up their situation;-

"The dead remembered – the living forgotten."

*A cushion by Painted Fabrics.*

It was at Wharncliffe War Hospital, at Middlewood, on the outskirts of Sheffield, that help came to these patients from a volunteer called Annie Bindon Carter, (1883-1969) who was accompanied by some of her friends.

Utilising their training from the Sheffield School of Art, the women started painting classes, three afternoons a week, as a form of occupational therapy for the men.

The ladies must have been very persuasive when they attached the paintbrushes to the remains of the soldiers healed, but missing limbs. Gently, they coaxed the patients to paint through the stencils onto the silks and fabrics, to create colourful and imaginative designs.

What they produced soon expanded into a business, which was first based at Snigg Hill in Sheffield.

What they made and sold, was a clever way of giving the men work with dignity, and to provide them with a source of income.

The business evolved to produce a range of goods including;- dresses, shawls, theatre backdrops, scarves, handkerchiefs, furnishing fabrics, coats, and leather work.

*Painted scarves*

**"Work not charity"** was the painted fabrics motto.

# Painted Fabrics Ltd. 1915 - 1959

In 1923, the land and huts at Norton, Woodseats, which formerly belonged to the old WAACS (Women's Auxiliary Army Corps), were purchased by the United Services Fund, and leased to Painted Fabrics Ltd.

On August the 8th 1925, the business officially opened, and received royal patronage from Princess Mary.

The work continued up to 1939, but the demand for the fabrics fell as World War II started, and the workshops were taken over for the production of aircraft parts. After the war, Painted Fabrics started again, but this time with the men injured from both world wars.

The years after the second world war, saw the introduction of national benefit schemes, and a rapidly changing fashion world. These factors affected a fall in demand, and the need for painted products.

*Commemorative plaque*

By 1959, it was decided that the business should close, and the business presented their archives with some work samples, to the Sheffield City Libraries for posterity.

To ensure that Painted Fabrics Ltd. and its people were not forgotten, a memorial plaque was installed on the 5th of August 2000, at Norton, on the site nearest to where the business started out. The plaque was unveiled by the great nephew and niece of Annie Bindon Carter O.B.E.

# Sheffield Top 12 Quiz

*This quiz and all the questions are connected to Sheffield in some way.*

**Your score:- under 5** correct (average)   **6-9** (good)   **10-12** (Tour guide)

**ANSWERS** - See page 55.

**1** — "By Wisdom and Courage" is the motto of which Sheffield football team?

**2** — What 1997 film, made in Sheffield, featured unemployed amateur striptease artists?

**3** — Who was the Queen that was imprisoned at Sheffield's Manor Lodge in the 1500's ?

**4** — What is the name of Sheffield's oldest bridge that spans the River Don?

**5** — What disaster hit Sheffield on 11th March 1864, killing over 200 people?

**6** — Which Sheffield actor, born on 17-4-59, has featured in Patriot Games and Golden Eye?

**7** — Sheffield's Crucible Theatre has hosted what World Championship since 1977?

**8** — Sheffield's Canal Basin was built between 1816-1819, and is now renamed as what?

**9** — Is the "Cutting Edge" steel sculpture found at;- Sheaf Square or Meadowhall?

**10** — Which monarch opened Sheffield's Town Hall on the 21st May 1897?

**11** — Sheffield takes its name partly from which river that flows through the city?

**12** — Who was born on 5 May 1943, in Sheffield, and was a member of Monty Python?

**"A can't get me breath" - I do not believe it!**

## Twin Towers    Tinsley    M1    J34

For many years, the two 250ft. high cooling towers, stood at the side of the M1's Tinsley viaduct. They were all that remained on the site of the demolished Blackburn Meadows Power Station.

Attempts to demolish them was staved off several times due to fears that the falling debris may damage the viaduct.

Even rare nesting birds helped to delay proceedings, but inevitably, the towers were demolished at 03:00 hours on 24th August 2008.

The public watched in safety from a specially provided viewing platform, so they could say their goodbye's to what was an iconic Sheffield landmark.

## The Don Valley Stadium    S9-3TL

Costing around £29 million to build, the stadium was opened in 1990, ready for the 1991, World Student Games.

It had a capacity for 25,000 people, and has been host to football, rugby, and live music performances.

Due to the cities budget cuts, it was closed, and demolition began in 2013, ending in May 2014.

## The Tramcar Pub - London Rd.

The pub was closed and demolished around 2005-6. It had a sing along bar in the back, and it was very popular with football fans. The pub is remembered for its beautifully painted image of tram number 512, that faced the oncoming traffic, on the corner of the building.

# Secret Snippets

The following pages are "Secret Snippets," which are a collection of unusual city observations. They include a post code, (when possible) so that you can visit these places for yourself.

The objects may have gone un-noticed by people for years, or is it the story behind them that is the secret?

No matter which, they are good fun to track down and say that you have seen them "up close and personal."

Shhh...

**Drakes Decent**          S20 7JJ
Drake house Retail Park

A cluster of three stainless steel Drakes created in 1998, by Walenty Pytel, are mounted on a pole amidst a hedged garden at the entrance to the retail park.

**Horse & Rider**    Fountain Precinct
(Barkers Pool)          S1 2JA

The 12ft. statue by David Wynne, has a memorial plaque nearby that states it was presented to the people of Sheffield by the family of the late Hyman Stone in his memory, and by Gauntlet Developments, who built the Fountain Precinct.

**The Winter Gardens**     S1 2LH
Surrey Street

This photo was taken in 2003, before the building of Saint Paul's hotel. It allows the full shape of this amazing structure to be viewed.

The laminated larch wood sections, create the uniquely shaped, strong, curved, roof supports (See inset photo)

Change is inevitable - except from a vending machine!

## The Beauchief Hotel      S7 2QW
Abbeydale road - Beauchief

This building was the hotel for the nearby railway station which was originally called Abbey Houses. The station later became the Beauchief & Abbeydale station.

The station closed on 1st January 1961, and its hotel became the Beauchief hotel.

The hotel has now closed, and its future is uncertain, but the station name over the main entrance door, can still be seen.

## The John Shortridge memorial    S2 3AE

John Shortridge was an engineer and industrialist, and was influential in the building of the Wicker Arches. He also introduced the first horse-drawn tram route from the town centre, to the Red Lion public house at Heeley. On his death in 1869, this memorial was built. It is found in the graveyard at Heeley Parish Church.

At over 2 tons, it took 20 horses to pull it up Sheaf Street. (now Gleadless Road)

## Cementation furnace      S3 7BD
Doncaster Street.

This is a Grade II listed building, and it is the only steel making furnace of its type to survive undamaged in Britain.

The furnace was used on Blister steel, which was the first type of commercially used steel. It was built in 1848, by a local steel firm;- Daniel Doncaster & Sons.

Operating throughout World War II, the furnace finally ceased steel production in 1951. The white flap on the top of the furnace, was used for air raid blackouts.

# Places to visit

**The Botanical Gardens**
Clarkehouse Road

Postcode - S10 2LN

**The Winter Gardens**
90, Surrey Street

Postcode - S1 2LH

**Bishops House**
Norton Lees Lane
Meersbrook Park

Postcode - S8 9BE

**The Town Hall Peace Gardens**
Pinstone Street

Postcode - S1 2HH

**Sheffield Cathedral**
Church Street

Postcode - S1 1HA

**Victoria Quays**
Wharf street

Postcode - S2 5SY

**Kelham Island**
Industrial Museum
Alma Street

Postcode - S3 8RY

**Car Park** - Milton St. S3 7WH

Its an odd place to visit but, Milton Street car park in the city centre, is home to some top quality graffiti by some of Sheffield's finest street artists.

Enjoy them while they are there, because they could disappear anytime...

"Well a'l gurra borrum o' our stairs" - I am surprised

# Yorkshire phrases to baffle folk

These words and phrases are fairly common in Yorkshire, or as we say "Gods chosen land," and they should be tried out on any willing visitor to the area, to see if they are as baffling to them as we think.

**Ear all, see all, say nowt.  Eat all, sup all, pay nowt.
And if ever thou does owt fer nowt – allus do it fer thissen.**

"Hear all, see all, say nothing. Eat all, drink all, pay nothing.
And if you ever do anything for nothing - always do it for yourself."

**Never buy owt wi' wudden 'andles cus it allus means 'ard work!**

Never buy anything with wooden handles because it always means hard work - (In particular gardening tools)

**Ey up! Never mind state o'place, cum in and sit thissen dahn, an' wi'l 'ave a reet good natter, an 'put world reet!**

Hello - Excuse the untidiness of my house, and come inside and sit yourself down and we will have a good talk, and sort out your problems.

### Seahorse or Dragon? - Town Hall
### Pinstone Street - S1 2HH

This controversial piece of stonework, is found in the arch above the Town Hall front doors.

Some people see it as a Sea Horse, whilst others see it as a Dragon.

Perhaps the argument for it being a Dragon is more plausible, because of the two stone carvings to the left and right of it called "Steam and Electricity."

It may be the combination of the steam, electricity, and the fire from the dragon, that represents the three main power sources needed to make steel?

The steel theme continues with other stone carvings found on the exterior walls of the Town Hall, including;-

Buffers, Smelters, Grinders, Miners, Ivory carvers, and other skilled trades. The stone carvings symbolise the pride the city has for its craftsmen.

### Jarvis Cocker poem;- S2 4QG
### The Forge - Boston Street.
### "Trashed on cider"

The 30 foot high poem on the side wall of The Forge, was a contribution in 2005, to the Off the shelf literary festival.

'Within these walls
the future may be
being forged
Or maybe
Jez is getting trashed
on cider
But when you melt
you become the shape
of your surroundings:
Your horizons
become wider.
Don't they teach
you no brains
at that school?'

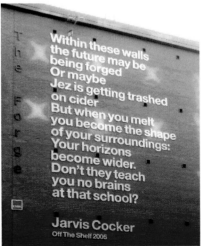

Within these walls
the future may be
being forged
Or maybe
Jez is getting trashed
on cider
But when you melt
you become the shape
of your surroundings:
Your horizons
become wider.
Don't they teach
you no brains
at that school?

Jarvis Cocker
Off The Shelf 2005

"Cum an get yer cha whileits ot!"
*Or - Come and get your tea whilst it is hot!*

It is not uncommon in Sheffield to be called "Duck" or "Love" especially if being served in a shop or dealing with a trader.
The common greeting and enquiry to how you can be assisted is;-
*"Ar tha allreet luv? - Can I elp yer?"*

In Sheffield we have "Fishcakes" for sale in our Chip Shops, which in other parts of the country may be called;- Fish Scallops, Fish Rissoles, or even Potato cakes.
The Sheffield version is;- two large slices of potato with fish pieces between them, which is then battered, and deep fried.
It is an excellent mini meal when put inside a bread cake, with salt and vinegar added.

**Cutlers' Hall** is a Grade II* listed.     S1 1HG
It is the headquarters of the Company of Cutlers in Hallamshire.

You may ask;-  why are there Elephants on the handles of the Cutlers Hall front doors?

The answer is quite simple when you think of what some cutlery handles were once made of - Ivory.

**Totley Tunnel East** - Signal box     S17 3QT
View this well-known local landmark from the rail bridge on Totley Brook Road.
 It is a type 2B signal box, and was built in 1893. It is the last survivor of four railway signal boxes in the Dore and Totley area.
It controls railway signals on the Manchester to Sheffield line, and the traffic through the 6,230 yard long,- Dore and Totley tunnel.

All over the city is street art, sculptures, wall paintings, and unusual objects. Most of them are in plain view to the public, but many of those listed here are not so easy to spot and admire, unless you know where they are. Here are just a small selection from the hundreds to see.

### THE PARKWAY MAN

He is located on the eastern side of Bowden Howsteads Wood at the junction of the Parkway A630 and the Mosbrough Parkway A57. Pedestrian access is along a wooded footpath via Richmond Park Crescent.

It is a cast iron sculpture of a steelworker holding a sledge hammer, which stands around 3 metre high, and weighs 3 tons.

It was sited here in 2001, and is a work by Jason Thompson.

The figure is mostly secluded by the trees in the summer, but becomes very visible in the winter to passing cars using the slip road to Mosborough from the Parkway.

### GREAT CONVERSATION     S8 9QL

This work is found on Brooklyn Road in the S8 area of Sheffield. It was painted by "Faunagraphic" whose work can be seen all over Sheffield. Her work principally focuses on birds and wildlife.

The mural painted onto this house side, is based upon a canvas called "Great Conversation."

It shows three green and yellow great tits, amongst flowers and viola leaves.

The mural took 3 days to complete, and was done in 3 stages. It is a vibrant and exciting work, and is very appropriate with Meersbrook Park opposite.

   " Tha's a reet dolls 'ead" - you are really stupid

## Steel Worker - Castle St.    S1 2AF

This brick mosaic is on the side of a building on Castle Street, and was created by Paul Waplington.

The city council commissioned the work in the 1980's, to commemorate the steel industry in Sheffield.

## Arundel Street    S1 2NT

This is a highly colourful and detailed wall mural by Foundry Art. It is on the side of the Arundel Joinery building which is on Arundel Street.

(Only part of the work is shown).

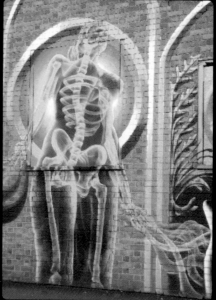

## Harry Brearley    S1 2LX
Howard St.

On the side of the Howard Hotel, is this 42 ft high tribute to Harry Brearley. He was the probable inventor of stainless steel.

The work was commissioned to mark the 100th anniversary of the discovery.

### The Four Vultures - Eyre Lane. S1

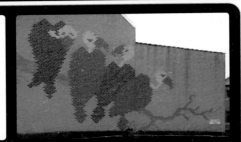

Not much is known of this work as it is not fully listed as a public work of art.

It is a brick mural possibly created by R. Bingham, and is dating from around 1980.

### The Castle House Man    S3 8LS
Angel Street

This sculpture of Vulcan (The god of steel) has been on Castle House since 1962.

It was created by Boris Tietze.

It was commissioned by a men's outfitter in the building, to mark the city's golden years of quality steel production.

### Face at the Window? Doncaster St.

There is not much known about this piece of art work, but it is surprising to see "someone" looking through a blocked up window in a large old building opposite the Cementation furnace.

It is a good opportunity to see two amazing things on one street.

### The Sheffield Foxes -    S8 area

These spray painted foxes, are in various colours, and are appearing around the Meersbrook and the Broadfield Road area of the city. This one was discovered on a cafe wall on Meersbrook Park Road.

The "foxy" artist is unknown.

## The Goodwin Fountain          S1 2HH

The fountain in Fargate, that stood from 1961 to 1998, was first dedicated to Alderman James Sterling, but was later officially known as the Goodwin Fountain. The new Goodwin fountain in the Peace Gardens, replaced the Fargate one, and has 89 walk-in jets.

## National Centre for Popular Music
Paternoster Row          S1 2QQ

The centre opened as a music and culture museum on 1st March 1999, but it closed in June 2000, due to low visitor numbers. What is unusual about these stainless steel units, is that they resemble a timpani drum, and have tops that are designed to slowly rotate with the wind direction.

## Mosaic    Abbeydale Road   S17 3LE

This mosaic is found on what was a church. During the first world war, it was used as a hospital, and it is now being used as a Mail Sorting Office.
The mosaic depicts the buildings use as a VAD (Voluntary Aid Detachment) hospital, that initially cared for Belgian soldiers injured in the war.

## Queens Road Retail Park.    S2 4DR

At the entrance to the retail park are two Alice in Wonderland sculptures;- "The Queen of Hearts" and the "Mad Hatter." They were carved on site, inside one of the vacant buildings, at the time, by Vega Bermejo in 1994.

# Rustless Steel?

Not far from Bramhall Lane football ground, on Randall Street, is Portland Works. People may pass this building unaware of its connection with "Rustless Steel" and its probable inventor;- Harry Brearley.

Brearley was working at Firth Brown's research laboratory as a metallurgist, when he discovered that when chromium was added to molten iron, the steel did not rust, and it was also resistant to acid attacks.

*Portland Works  S2 4SJ*

The new type of steel was smelted on 13th of August 1913, and it was Brearley who immediately saw the potential for this new steel in the cutlery industry. Brearley had great difficulty persuading his employers, so to prove his point, he had some knives made at a local cutler's, R.F. Mosley & Co. at Portland Works. Under his and the works managers supervision, the new cutlery was made and sent out to their friends for testing.

There were favourable results from this trial, with no returns.

Brearley called it "Rustless steel," but it was Ernest Stuart the cutlery manager of Mosley's, who was the first to refer to the new knives as "stainless" in order to make them more marketable.

*So perhaps 'Stainless Steel' was born in Portland Works!*

The delay and hesitance of Brearley's employers to patent the discovery in the United Kingdom, led to the process being first registered in Germany. Brearley found that it had not been patented and registered in the USA, so in 1921, he visited the USA to act as a witness over his patent rights. During the registration, Firth & Brown Steels undermined his case, by insisting that the patent was theirs because Brearley was their employee.

Although Harry Brearley had been awarded the Iron and Steel Institute's Bessemer Gold Medal in 1920, and eventually became a director of Brown Bayley in 1925, he was never awarded the ownership of his discovery.

His new chromium steel, formed the basis for a wide range of stainless and special steels, which are now used across the world.

Portland Works was awarded Grade II listed status by English Heritage in 1995, and was subsequently upgraded to Grade II* listed status in 2007. The building has workshop areas that demonstrate the use of power in the cutlery manufacturing process, and also hand forging and steam grinding rooms. Portland Works is currently utilised as a centre for craftsmen, artists, and small manufacturing businesses.

* The chimney stack was reduced in height during the second world war, to prevent it from being used for enemy aircraft direction finding.

# Dus tha know?

Dus tha know? or Do you know? (When translated) that the following stories are from Sheffield people, who at the time, accepted these things as a normal way of life.

Today, younger readers may think some of these secrets of Sheffield life hard to believe or bizarre.

---

*During World War II, Britain was being slowly starved by the German and Axis powers sinking our supply ships. It was a desperate situation with food running short, so the Allied nations sent canned food to the grateful British people. It had a personal letter around the can, with a message of hope.*

**A Letter to Someone in Great Britain**

From a Friend in New South Wales, Australia

*Dear Friend – please accept this gift of food as a token of our admiration for your courage and fortitude, and the sacrifices you are still making; Sacrifices which show you are an example to the world in peace as well as war...*

(New South Wales)

***

*We lived in back to back houses at Darnall at a time when gambling was illegal. I remember "runners" collecting bets along the streets from people's houses. The runner would go to the backyard fence of the "Bookies" house, and rattle it in a certain way. The "Bookie" would come from his house and take the bets.*
(N)

***

*Just after WWII, in Manor Lane, some prefabricated houses were being built to house those who were "Bombed out." I remember as a child, that German prisoner of war labour was used to lay the concrete foundations for the new houses.*

*One German in particular called "Otto," used to build children's toys from old tea chests and bits of wood that he could find. He made some great toys and gave them to us. He gave me a pull along sausage dog on wheels and a bat with a nodding chicken on it.*
(Neil)

***

*When I was a little girl, and there was a bombing raid on, my uncle would take our minds of it by getting us to knit dish cloths.*
(Jean)

---

**" Gerrus sum more coyl will tha?" - Fetch more coal will you?**

*I worked as an apprentice joiner for a Sheffield steeplejack company called W.E.Harrison that was just off Glossop Road. The company was established in 1854.*

*I was told the company was made famous through Mr. Harrison's steeplejack skills. He was once sought by the Navy league, to decorate Nelson's column in London for Trafalgar day, in the year 1896.*

*He achieved this task by lashing ladders to the column with a series of taut ropes.*

*It was completed without any damage or drilling of the 180 foot high monument.*

*The wiring and decorations weighed nearly seven tons, and it was hoisted up to the top by pulleys.*                    *(N.B)*

*W.E.Harrison - Steeplejacks*

***

*I remember the police using this box next to the Town Hall when I was a young lad.*

*On occasions you would hear the telephone bell inside ring.*

*It has always reminded me of Dr.Who's Tardis, but today I know it is equally special, because it is the last surviving Police Box of its type from 120 that was installed in South Yorkshire.*                    *(Chris)*

*Police Box - Surrey Street*

***

*During WW II, rationing made women's beauty products, make up and nylons, very difficult to get hold of. Women started to improvise by using beetroot as a lip stain, and gravy browning or cold tea dregs to dye their legs to look like nylon stockings.*

*They completed the illusion of wearing nylons, by drawing lines up the back of their legs using eyebrow pens. Hitler hated cosmetics, so it made them feel even better at the Saturday night dance.*          *(Irene)*

**"A'm completely jiggered" - I am completely exhausted**

# Ghostly Sheffield

If you believe in ghosts, haunting's or definitely not, Sheffield has some stories to tell. Here are just a few, and we leave it up to you to decide.

**Manor Lodge**  Manor lane  S2 1UL

The ghost of Mary Queen of Scots is said to haunt the Turret House.

Strange happenings in the building were recorded during the 1930's, by the caretakers.

They tell of a lady, dressed all in black, gliding across the floor, and she could disappear into the walls.

There was also an unexplained event, when a heavy incense burner moved its position - on its own?

**Bunting Nook**  S8 8JW

This haunting is about two eloping lovers who were thrown off their horse in the lane, and the fall broke both of their necks.

It is said that their ghosts now haunt the lane where no bird is said to sing.

This may be an odd thing to say when the lane is named after a type of bird;- a Bunting?

**Carbrook Hall**  S9 2FJ

In this hall, it has been reported that the ghost of Colonel Bright, who was a close friend of Oliver Cromwell, has been seen standing at the top of the stair landing.

There are other haunting's here, including the sound of children, an elderly woman from the 1920's, a Roundhead, a monk, and a ghostly figure throwing things around the bar.

"It's right nice!" - Yorkshire for;- It is really nice

The first sighting of this phenomenon was in London in 1837, and more followed later in the Midlands and in Scotland.

People claimed that this "creature" could take great leaps, had claws and red eyes, so its fame spread quickly to other parts of the country. It was even featured at the time in the "Penny Dreadful" comic books, with the nickname:- "Spring Heeled Jack."

In Sheffield, there was a strikingly similar report of a "Park Ghost" that was first seen around April 1873, and was said to be haunting the Cholera Monument Grounds next to Clay Woods. *(See page footnote)*

Witnesses described "him" as very tall, gaunt, and dressed all in white. He had an unearthly and supernatural aspect about him, and was sometimes seen to hover or skim over the ground. He was also able to make huge leaps into the air, and to bound over very high walls with ease.

The numerous sightings, and the behaviour of the "Park Ghost" was later identified by the locals to be;- "Spring Heeled Jack."

*Spring Heeled Jack*

There were more reported attacks by "Jack," from the Arbourthorne and Sky Edge districts of the city, and his bizarre antics spread fear and terror throughout Sheffield.

For months, vigilante groups armed with sticks tried to capture the creature, but it always eluded them.

Gradually over the years, the attacks and sightings diminished, and "Spring Heeled Jack" slowly faded into local legend.

However it is worth noting, that the last alleged sighting of him was as recent as the 1970's, when he was seen climbing over the rooftops in the Attercliffe area of Sheffield.

*The Cholera Monument*

## Queen Victoria's Statue    S11 7AA
(Endcliffe Park)

It may be assumed that the monument to Queen Victoria and her associated statues "Maternity" and "Labour," has always been in Endcliffe park, but in fact it was first unveiled by Princess Beatrice in Town Hall Square on 11th May 1905. (Town Hall Square as it was known then, is the junction of Barkers Pool, Pinstone Street, Surrey Street and Fargate.)

Because of the city centre changes, it was decided to move the statue by lorry to its current position, on 24th February 1930.

## The Lycopod - Botanical gardens  S10 2LN

This is the fossilised stump and roots of a Giant Club Moss or Lycopod, which is about 300 million years old. It was found during the excavation of the foundations for Sheffield Midland Station. It can be viewed in the Evolution Garden, which is an area favoured by squirrels, as you can just see.

Inside the Robert Marnock Garden, is a giant leaf cutter ant sculpture, made from stainless steel called "ANTHEA".
It was created by the sculptor Johnny White, and was sited in the garden in 2008.

## Hunters Bar - Toll gate    S11 8HY

These gateposts are found in the centre of Hunters Bar roundabout signifying that it was once the site of a toll gate into the city.

The last toll duty here was paid by a Mr W.H. Haigh, who passed through the gate just prior to midnight on 31 October, 1884.
Coincidentally, he was also the first person to pass through the gate without any charge.

## Weston Park Bandstand          S10 2TP

It has been in Weston Park since the early 1900's and is hardly a secret, but what may not be known, is that It was designed in 1874 by Flockton and Gibbs the Sheffield architects, and was built in a foundry in Glasgow. It is the last surviving Victorian Bandstand in a Sheffield park, and was one of a pair, the other being in Hillsborough Park, (Now demolished). The bandstand was in use until the mid 1970's, and is now an approved civil wedding venue.

## Gas Street Lamp - Cemetery Rd    S11 8AU

This "Sewer Gas Destructor Lamp" as it is called, was one of 82 lamps that were installed in Sheffield in the late 1800's to burn off the build-up of methane and other gases generated in the cities sewers. The lamps were strategically placed in areas where gas was likely to collect.

In the lamp hood, are three mantles, which burn the gas at an intense heat, forming an up draught through the burner column.

The methane gas is safely burnt off, and at night, the lamps also provide some street lighting.

The lamps are Grade II listed, and at this point in time, there are around 20 of them left in Sheffield.

## Brightside Colliery Memorial Wheel
Holywell Road - Sheffield 4

There were two colliery shafts in this area, and Colliery Road still exists nearby.
The memorial wheel pays tribute to the men who worked at the pit, and to those men who died at the pit through accidents.

# Secret Snippets

**The Blue Lantern -** Norfolk Park S2 2PL Granville Road Entrance.

The 12th Duke of Norfolk started the design layout of the 30 hectare park (which is now known as the Norfolk Heritage Park) in 1841.
It was completed under the guidance of the 13th Duke in 1848. The park was one of the first in the country to offer free admission to the public.

On Granville Road in front of the park entrance gates, is this ornate blue, five lantern street lamp. The lamp was sited here in 1904, and it is Grade II listed.

**Guide for Amphibians** S11 7AA Endcliffe Park (near to the cafe.)

The inset picture is of a smaller wood carving on this site by Jason Thomson which was commissioned in 1997, called:- 'A Feeled Guide to Amphibians.'
It has now been replaced by the larger more permanent sculpture.

**Marilyn Monroe -** Norton S8 7UJ Meadowhead.

This figurine is seen with a clock, soldier, and other objects, on the external parapet above the entrance to a wine shop at Meadowhead.

It's fun to see and to remember that one of Marilyn's famous quotes was;- *"Give a girl the right shoes, and she can conquer the world."*

" Thas not back'ard at comin for'ard" - you are being pushy

### "Mi Amigo" Memorial - Endcliffe Park

The memorial stone marks the crash site of the USAAF B-17 Flying Fortress "Mi Amigo."

On 22 February 1944, the aircraft was returning home, and badly damaged, from a bombing run over Denmark.

The pilot;- Lieutenant J. Kriegshauser, saw children in the park playing, and rather than crash amongst them, he sacrificed the 10 man crew by landing in the trees behind the cafe.

He was posthumously awarded the US. Distinguished Flying Cross for his courage.

In 1969, on the hillside behind the cafe, ten American oaks were planted to honour each member of the crew.

### The Stepping Stones          S11 7AA
Endcliffe Park

These stepping stones are sometimes missed on the way to the cafe.

They have been here for years, and offer a dry crossing across the Porter Brook. They are great fun to cross, but take a towel;- just in case.

### Saint Cyprian's Church        S12 4SX

This stone carving over the west door, celebrates the link between Saint Cyprian's church and Saint James church at Derwent. It depicts the spire of the submerged church of St. James below the new Ladybower Reservoir.

The spire was seen protruding above the waters of the new reservoir for some years before it was removed

# Secret Snippets

### White Lion Hotel      S2 4HT
Chesterfield Road.

The White Lion on Chesterfield Road was established in 1781, and its exterior is tiled and very decorative, but take a look at the letters on the front window.

I suspect the ales are excellent, if you look closely at the letter "N" in Windsor.

### Heeley Tramcar depot      S8 9QW

This building, built in 1878, for horse drawn trams, has an interesting secret.

When the new flats behind it were built, the archway was demolished for ease of access. Sheffield Council ordered that the arch had to be rebuilt, using all the original material. It was, and the building is now Grade II listed.

### Henderson's Relish      S3 7RD

Henderson's Relish, is a local delicacy, that is seldom found outside Yorkshire.

The "sauce" was made here from the late 1800's, until 2013. The production was then moved to a new site near the city's Parkway. There are some plans for this treasured landmark to become a pub, and for it to keep its original signs.

### The Bochum Bell      S1 2HH

The Bochum bell is found in a flower bed in Sheffield's Peace Garden, on Pinstone Street.

It was presented in 1986, to the people of Sheffield, on the 35th anniversary of the cities twinning of Sheffield and Bochum in Germany, in 1950.

Recently, an old Henderson's relish bottle was unearthed at "The Somme."

# Secret Snippets

## The Blue Police Lamp    S8 0SL
Woodseats

Blue lamps appeared outside British police stations from 1861, and spread throughout the British Empire. Some of these symbols of British policing still remain, and have even appeared in films such as;- "The Blue Lamp."

## The Tilt Hammer    S7 2QW
Abbeydale Industrial Museum

At the entrance to the museum is a Drop or Tilt hammer.
It was driven by water power, and was used to forge hot metal into shape for tools such as:- Scythes, knives, and a range of agricultural implements.

## Highfield Library    S2 4NF
Above the main door of the library is this quotation by Thomas Carlyle:-

*That there should one man die ignorant who had capacity for knowledge, this I call a tragedy, were it to happen more than twenty times in the minute, as by some computations it does.*

Basically it means;- the provision of knowledge, for free, to those who are in poverty and toil.

## The Spiders web    S4 7UQ

This unusual artwork by Johnny White dated (1994-5) is found on the exterior wall of the System Gripple factory, at the corner of Firth Drive and Saville Street. The spiders steel web is held in place using one of the companies own products;- "Gripple."

*Top Left:-* **Water Fountain**
Meersbrook Park          S8 9FL

*Top right:-* **Knot Sculpture**
Spital Hill -   Burngreave Road

*Bottom Left:-* **Hop Sculpture**
Ecclesall Rd. at the old Wards
Brewery.          S11 8HW

*Bottom Right:-* **The 3 Bears**
Whirlow Brook Park   S11 9QD

## Cobweb Bridge      S1 2AB

This unique bridge is accessible from Blonk street, or the Wicker, and has "spiders" in the roof arch.

It hangs over the River Don on a "steel web." The bridge is part of the 8km. long Five Weir Walk trail along the River Don, which starts in the city centre, and ends at Meadowhall.

## Water Pump      S8 8QA

Found near the top of Cobnar Rd. and Bole Hill. (footpath access only)

The water pump is now disused. It is a remnant from when this area was a small village. People at that time, had to pump the water by hand, and carry it home in a bucket.

## 1933 Signpost - Hathersage Road & Hidden transmitter mast.

Just across from Limb Lane is a signpost dating from 1933.

As you walk uphill, away from the city, you may have never noticed the cleverly disguised transmitter mast, with its "evergreen" plastic leaves?

## The Time Signal      S1 2GZ
Barkers Pool on Yorkshire House

From 1874, the one o'clock time signal was relayed from Greenwich to H. L. Browns office. It sounded daily so that people in the city centre could set their watches accurately. The sign and siren are shown here.

**Snow Gates** - Saxon Road - Heeley - S8

This is not just a decorative gate, but one of the three "snow gates" here. They allow snow to be emptied easily into the River Sheaf, which flows behind them.
The inscription on the gate says:-
*"Balance is the key to life struggling to keep sane, to tear it with a knife would make the balance turn to rain."*

**Eagle** - Beauchief Abbey Cottages   S8

This lectern style Eagle is found on the parapet of a cottage near to Beauchief Abbey.
Why it's there is not known, and it may be just ornamental, but coincidentally, Saint John the Evangelist used the symbol of an eagle to spread the gospel, and St. Johns church is nearby on Abbeydale Road. Who knows? - but it is fun to see.

**Standard Measure**                S1 2HN

The Standard Measures were put in a public place as an early type of consumer protection. By being there, they quickly resolved most trading disputes.
For several centuries, these measures were in St. Paul's parade, but in 1998, they were relocated to Cheney Row.

**Children's Shelter** Norfolk St.    S1 2JE

Emerson Bainbridge who was a mining engineer, J.P. and philanthropist, funded the Jeffie Bainbridge children's shelter on the death of his wife. Not only was this a memorial to her, but it provided help for the waif and stray children in the town.
It was opened on 28/12/1894, by the Duke & Duchess of Portland.

### Alfred Beckett Works - Ball Street    S3

Brooklyn Works were constructed in the mid 19th century for the firm of Alfred Beckett, who was a manufacturer of steel, saws, and files. Alfred Beckett & Sons Ltd. continued to manufacture at the Brooklyn Works until the mid-1960s, using the "Matchless" trademark.

### The Jeffcock Memorial    S13 9BP
Water trough & drinking fountain

The memorial fountain is Grade II listed, and dates from 1900. It is made from moulded grey and pink granite.

This is a multi function fountain, that combines a horse trough, with two small troughs below it for dogs.

It also has a drinking bowl with an arched opening, for thirsty travellers to use.

### Columbia Place    Suffolk Rd.    S2 4AR

The building was erected in 1849, as a steel and file works, but it actually looks like an embassy. The large royal coat of arms was fitted on the building in 1868, by the owners of the property, William Wigfall & sons, who were brush manufacturers. Currently, the building is used as flats.

### The Pill Box - Hecla    (Five Weir Walk)
Near to the B6083

This remnant from WWII, was built to protect the munitions works at Hecla.

It can be found on the Five Weir Walk route, near to the Newhall Road Bridge.

Nearby is Attercliffe Cemetery, which contains some very old graves.

# Secret Snippets

## Fulwood Chapel & stocks    S10 4GL

The chapel was was built as a meeting house for English Dissenters, and was completed in 1729, at a cost of £75.

In 1929, during a road widening scheme, a garden in front of the chapel was removed, and the village stocks were placed in front of the building. The chapel and stocks are Grade II listed.

## St James Church    Norton    S8 8JQ

Outside St. James Church, is this very decorative horse trough dating from 1905. In 1956, it was moved from its original site near the water tower, when the new roundabout was being built.

It is dedicated to Annie Hall, the wife of George Walker Hall, who was the last Vicar and first modern Rector of Norton.

## Spirit of Parkwood Springs    S5 8XB
Shirecliffe Rd / Cooks Wood Road.

In Parkwood Springs is an unusual steel sculpture by Jason Thomson, which stands facing the road. It was inspired by the park areas history, geology, and wildlife.

Nearby, and by the same artist is;-

### The Boy and the Bird    Rutland Rd.

On the hill top, nestled in woodland on the left hand side, is a child wearing a pair of oversized gloves sat on a bird's back. It represents Parkwood's industrial past and future. The Kestrel is clutching a Stanley hammer in homage to the former Stanley works.

# Cryptic Quiz

This quiz is a cryptic one, with clues relating to the districts of Sheffield. Perhaps some lateral thinking is needed to get the answers?
Rate your score below, and the answers are on page 55 if you need them.

**Q 1.** A District:- An annoyed clergyman lives here?

**Q 2.** A District:- Where they have trimmed their privets too much?

**Q 3.** A District:- A place to find dark coloured pebbles?

**Q 4.** A District:- Coal extraction in a wide open space?

**Q 5.** A District:- An old motor bike using a mallet?

**Q 6.** A District:- Angry water collected here?

**Q 7** A District:- Questions a birth?

**Q 8.** A District:- Set on fire then mourns over it?

**Q 9** A District:- Learned and knowledgeable gathering of trees?

**Q 10.** A District:- Common road vehicle joins a small river?

**Q 11.** A District:- Famous steel maker in a recreation area?

**Q 12.** A District:- Jogging at speed in wide open spaces?

**Q 13.** A District:- Skilful gain for a company is put in a safe place?

**Q 14.** A District:- Sowing everything here?

**Q 15.** A District:- A place for optimists?

Your score rating:-

**1-5  Hopeless**          **6-10  Very good**          **11-15  Awesome**

# Dus tha know?

**What is this?**    Greystones    S11

It is on the corner of Highcliffe Road and Greystones Road, and this old object may be the last of its type found in Sheffield?

**Clue**:- It has air holes around the top of the lid, to let the heat out.

**Answer**:- It's an old type of electrical transformer which was manufactured by the British Electric Transformer company. They were fitted to boost the mains power to homes at the far end of a long supply line. These rare items will disappear completely as the national power grid is upgraded.

**Hidden** in a small secluded area in a Sheffield golf club car park, is this relic from the "Cold War."

The crumbling steel and concrete is all that can be seen (above ground) of the small Royal Observer Corps (ROC) monitoring post. The main rooms are buried six foot below.

Around 1,500 were built in the UK to measure nuclear blast waves and monitor radioactive fallout.

Now, only about 70 of these remain.

**The Landsdowne Theatre**    S2 4LA

The theatre opened in Dec. 1914, and was used as a theatre until Dec. 1940. From the 1950's, the building has been called;- Locarno, Tiffany's, The Palais, The Music Factory, Club Generation, and The Bed nightclub. It is currently a supermarket.

   *" Ar' tha gunna go t' flicks toneet?"* - Are you going to the cinema tonight?

## The corner of Moore St. & Young St.
### S1 4UP

This building dates from 1906, and was the Joseph Pickering and Sons carton factory. It was purpose built for cartons and other products that were made here up to the late 1980's.

Shortly after, the business decided to move premises, and the building was sold. It is now a modern office block, which still retains its listed ornate terra cotta façade, that is well worth seeing.

## "Father and Daughter" post boxes
Surrey Street. **S1 2LG**

These postboxes are George V and Elizabeth II, so Father and Daughter! During the suffragette campaign, the George V post box was firebombed to raise the profile of the women's cause.

## Central Library   Surrey St.   S1 1XZ

You may have wondered why there is an Egyptian scribe carved in stone, high up on the corner of the building? It is there to symbolise - "knowledge."

It was carved from Portman stone by F. Tory & Sons of Ecclesall Road.

**"Put t' wood int' oil."** The origin of this phrase began many years ago when doors did not have locks. Doors were secured by putting a wooden bar across the door, into a hole in the door jamb. In Yorkshire, the phrase is still used, but when someone leaves the door open, and lets a cold draught in.

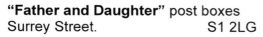

# Just good to see Quest

This collection of Sheffield snippets are just great to go and see, and are listed in no particular order.

If you make finding them a family quest, then you will need to plan, research, and time how long you take to get them all.

Use the time box on page 51, and Good Luck!

## A
### Hatfields Jaguar
*Postcode - S11 8ZD*

## B
### The Dore Stone
*S17 Dore village green*

## C
### Riverside Pub (Art)
*Postcode - S3 8EN*

## D
### Botanical Gardens
*Postcode - S10 2LN*

## E
### Cutting Edge
*Sheaf Square*

HINT;- Find tree face near to the Botanical Gardens lodge...

**F**   **Drop Hammer**   *Atlas* ☐

**G**   **VR Post Box**   *Cathedral* ☐

**H**   **Wall Art**   *Broad Street* ☐

**I**   **Lamp 1 of 3**   *Globe works* ☐

**J**   **Fountain**   *Broad Lane* ☐

**K**   **1777 hopper**   *Paradise Sq.* ☐

**L**   **Bill & Ben**   *Woodhouse* ☐

**M**   **Stanch**   *S1 4EG* ☐

**N**   **The Norton**   *S8 7UD* ☐

'As tha got the lot? Record your time here... ☐

# Bygone Sheffield

The following photographs of Sheffield are a selection from days gone by. We hope they bring back some happy memories of how it once was.

*The bottom of Dixon Lane in the 1960's*

*The Parkway - single carriageway*

*Gleadless valley in the 1970's*

*"Potters" / Cinema  at Heeley 2004*

*Steel making using the Drop Hammer*

*Western Bank*

*Canal Basin in the 1960's*

*The building of Park Square*

*James Mason (actor) at the building of the Crucible Theatre*

*Tram 279 Abbey Lane*

*Gatecrasher One club fire 2007*

# It happened that way!

The Wicker and West Street "dashes" were very popular in the 1970's. You would be amazed at how many pubs you could visit back then. We would drink a half pint of beer and get our card "stamped." When the card was full you sent off for a free "Tetley T-shirt." We almost did it in one night, but what a hangover next morning... *(Vin)*

We had some great nights at the Hofbrauhaus on Eyre Street. We would drink "Steins" of beer to the music of the Oompa Band. Singing Eins - ziga zig – Zwei - ziga zig – Zuffer (I never new what it all meant) but sang it anyway while standing and swaying on the table tops... *(Chris)*

In the 1950's, when working inside a file factory in Holme lane, one worker there said that he could work so fast he could do a weeks work in three days. Yes, he was like lightning, but paid the price with crippling arthritis in both legs due to water splashing off the files. *(Neil)*

When we were kids, we would come home from school starving.
We would cut off a slice of bread and put either butter or condensed milk on it, and sometimes we would sprinkle sugar on it. I think the kids were happier back then, and content with simple pleasures. *(Pauline)*

I can remember making a phone call, using this old style telephone box in Surrey Street, and using old penny coins, and pressing buttons A & B to connect the call. (CW)

**At one time... A Sheffield grinder's average life span was 30-35 years.**